DARE TO DESIRE

AN INVITATION TO FULFILL
YOUR DEEPEST DREAMS

JOHN ELDREDGE

ACKNOWLEDGEMENTS

Grateful acknowledgement is made to Thomas Nelson Publishers
for permission to reprint from the following books.

Eldredge, John. 2001. *Wild at Heart: Discovering the Secret of a Man's Soul.*
Nashville, Tennessee: Thomas Nelson Publishers.

Eldredge, John. 2000. *The Journey of Desire: Searching for the Life We've Only Dreamed Of.*
Nashville, Tennessee: Thomas Nelson Publishers.

Eldredge, John. 1997. *The Sacred Romance: Drawing Closer to the Heart of God.*
Nashville, Tennessee: Thomas Nelson Publishers.

Project editor: Kathy Baker
Design: UDG | DesignWorks

ISBN: 0-8499-9591-4

Printed and bound in the United States of America

www.thomasnelson.com

CONTENTS

DESIRE IS THE

ESSENCE OF THE HUMAN

SOUL, THE SECRET OF OUR

EXISTENCE. ABSOLUTELY

NOTHING OF HUMAN

GREATNESS IS EVER

ACCOMPLISHED WITHOUT IT.

AN INVITATION

THERE IS A DESIRE WITHIN EACH OF US,

IN THE DEEP CENTER OF OURSELVES

THAT WE CALL OUR HEART.

WE WERE BORN WITH IT, IT IS NEVER

COMPLETELY SATISFIED, AND IT

NEVER DIES. . . . OUR TRUE IDENTITY,

OUR REASON FOR BEING, IS TO BE

FOUND IN THIS DESIRE.

—GERALD MAY

IT'S NOT THAT

WE HAVE DESIRE—

WE ARE DESIRE

There is a secret set within each of our hearts. It often goes unnoticed. We rarely can put words to it, and for the most part it remains hidden in the deepest part of us.

It is simply our desire for life as it was *meant* to be.

Isn't there a life you have been searching for all your days? You might not always be aware of your search, and there are times when you seem to have abandoned looking altogether. But again and again it returns, this yearning that cries out for the life we prize. It is elusive, to be sure. It seems to come and go at will. Seasons may pass until it surfaces again. And though it seems to taunt us or even cause us great pain, we know when it returns that it is priceless. For if we could recover this desire, unearth it from beneath all distractions and embrace it as our deepest treasure, we would discover the secret of our existence.

You see, life comes to all of us as a mystery. We all share the same dilemma—we long for life and we're not sure where to find it. We wonder if we ever do find it, can we make it last? Our days come to us as a riddle, and the answers aren't handed out with our birth certificate.

Who am I, really?

Where will I find life?

What am I here for?

These are the deepest questions of the human heart. They are why we must *journey* to find the life we

The clue as to who we really are and why we are here comes to us through our heart's desire.

prize. It might surprise you to hear that the guide you have been given is the desire set deep within, the desire you often overlook, or mistake for something else or even choose to ignore.

But it's true. The clue as to who we really are and why we are here comes to us through our heart's *desire*.

Now, the life of our heart is a place of great mystery.

What I mean by "heart" is far, far more than just emotions and feelings. We describe a person without compassion as "heartless," and we urge him to "have a heart." Our deepest hurts we call "heartaches." Jilted lovers are "brokenhearted." Courageous soldiers are "bravehearted." The truly evil are "black-hearted," and a saint has a "heart of gold." If we need to speak at the most intimate level, we ask for a "heart-to-heart" talk. "Lighthearted" is how we feel on vacation. But when we lose our passion for life, we confess, "My heart's just not in it."

An ancient Jewish proverb describes the heart as "the wellspring of life" within us (Proverbs 4:23, NIV). Out of this wellspring flows all true caring and meaningful work, all real worship and all sacrifice. Our faith, hope, and love issue from this fount as well. In other words, anything that makes a life worth living flows out of your deep heart.

Your heart is simply the deepest, truest you.

It is the person you were meant to be if life had gone the way it was meant to go.

Think for a moment about your favorite movies— the ones that took your breath away, the ones you perhaps own now, or have seen many times. *Why* do you love

them? What does the hero or the heroine have that you would love to have?

I think you'll find that in the heart of every man is the desire for a battle to fight, an adventure to live, and a beauty to rescue. Look at the movies men love: *Shane, High Noon,* the *Rocky* films, *Chariots of Fire, Top Gun, Braveheart, Gladiator.* These box office hits speak to a man's heart, something core to who he is and what he longs for. Battle, adventure, and a beauty—these are what make a man come alive.

And what about films like *Titanic, The Princess Bride, Casablanca, Gone with the Wind, Sleepless in Seattle, Sense and Sensibility, Little Women?* Men didn't put those films at the top of the charts. No, they speak to a woman's deepest longings—to be pursued and fought for, to be swept up in a great adventure, to be the beauty. Isn't it true? These are the desires make a woman come alive.

In the long run, it doesn't matter how well we perform or what we accomplish—a life without heart is not worth living. To lose heart is to lose everything.

And a "loss of heart" best describes most men and women in our day. It isn't just the addictions and affairs and depression and heartaches, though, God knows, there is enough of those to cause even the best of us to lose heart. There's the *busyness*, the striving, the fact that most of us live merely to survive.

Most of us live out a script that someone else wrote for us.

Our lives are a collection of others' expectations. While we give the energy of our lives trying to fulfill the expectations of parents, teachers, employers, lovers and mentors, we lose track of the life of our own deep heart.

Think for a moment—how has life turned out differently than you thought it would? If you are single, did you want to be? If married, is this the marriage you hoped for? Do you long to have children or, in having them, are you delighted with the courses of their lives? Your friendships—are they as rich and deep and lasting as you want?

How about your work, your place in the world? Do you go to bed each night with a sense of having made a lasting contribution? Do you enjoy ongoing recognition for your unique successes? Are

you even working in a field that fits you? Are you working at all?

Bringing our heart along in our life's journey is the most important mission of our lives—and the hardest. It all turns on what we do with our desire.

If you'll have a look around, you will see that most people have abandoned the journey. They have lost heart. They are camped in places of resignation, or indulgence, or trapped in prisons of despair. I understand; I have frequented all those places myself. Life provides any number of reasons and occasions to abandon desire.

But by the grace of God, we cannot quite ever get rid of our desire.

In the quiet moments of the day we sense a nagging within, a discontentment, a hunger for something else. You see, even while we are "getting on with life," we keep an eye out for the life we secretly want. We can never entirely give up our quest.

It's not that we have desire—we *are* desire.

Desire is the essence of the human soul, the secret of our existence. Absolutely nothing of human greatness is ever accomplished without it. Not a symphony has been written, a mountain climbed, an injustice fought, or a love sustained apart from desire. Desire fuels our search for the life we prize.

We cannot solve the riddle of our existence, nor can we find the answer to our deepest questions without these deepest desires of our heart.

That's why the greatest human tragedy of all is to abandon the desires of your heart, to give up searching for life. For in those hidden desires, you will discover the person you were meant to be and the life you were meant to live.

The secret of your life is written on your heart's desire.

And the time has come to return to the journey.

Wherever you are, whatever you are doing, you can pick up the trail. Desire is the map you have been given to find the only life worth living. And so I offer this book as an invitation to a daring and marvelous journey—a quest in search of the life God meant for you to live, the man or the woman he created you to be. It is a rare and difficult journey, but a deeply thrilling one as well . . . a journey of *desire*.

MIDDLE
OF NOWHERE

IN THE MIDDLE OF THE

ROAD OF MY LIFE,

I AWOKE IN A DARK WOOD,

WHERE THE TRUE WAY WAS

WHOLLY LOST.

—ALIGHIERI DANTE

It's Common for
Our Journey to Begin
With a Sense of
Discontent, or of
Being Lost.

S ome years into our life's journey, a voice speaks to us amidst all we are doing.

Something is missing.

The voice often comes in the middle of the night or the early hours of the morning, when our hearts are most unedited and vulnerable.

At first, we mistake the source of this voice and assume it is just our imagination. We fluff up our pillow, roll over, and go back to sleep. Days, weeks, even months go by and the voice speaks to us again:

Aren't you thirsty? Listen to your heart. You long to be in a love affair, an adventure. You were made for something more. You know it.

It's common for our journey to begin with a sense of discontent, or of being lost.

Starting very early, you see, life teaches all of us to ignore and distrust the deepest yearnings of our heart. Life instructs us to suppress our longings and live only in the external world where efficiency and performance are everything. We learn from parents and peers, at school, at work, and even from our spiritual mentors that our heart—the deepest truest us—isn't wanted.

Instead, we are wanted for what we can offer functionally. If rich, we are honored for our wealth, if beautiful, for our looks, if intelligent, for our brains. So we learn to offer only those parts of us that are approved, living out a careful performance to gain acceptance.

We divorce ourselves from our heart and live a double life.

The external life is what everyone sees—the life of work and play and church, of family and friends, of paying bills and growing older. Bob is an accountant; Mary works for the government; Ted is an attorney. Here, in the external life,

busyness substitutes for meaning,
efficiency substitutes for creativity,
and functional relationships substitute for love.

In the outer life we live from *ought*—I ought to do this—rather than from *desire*—I want to do this.

Think about how a man's life unfolds nowadays. Endless hours at a computer screen; selling shoes at the mall; meetings, memos, phone calls. Corporate policies and procedures are designed with one aim: to harness a man to the plow and make him produce efficiently.

But the soul refuses to be harnessed; it knows nothing of daytimers and deadlines and financial statements. The soul longs for passion, for freedom, for *life*.

Can a man live all his days just being punctual and productive? Is that what little boys dream of? Is that what *you* dreamed of?

So we learn to offer only those parts of us that are approved, living out a careful performance to gain acceptance.

Most men in the church seem to believe that God put them on the earth to be good boys. The problem with men, we are told, is that they don't know how to keep their promises, be spiritual leaders, talk to their wives, or raise their children. But, if they will try hard they can reach the lofty summit of becoming a really nice guy. Now, male readers, in all your boyhood dreams, did you ever dream of just becoming a nice guy?

Ladies, was the prince of your dreams dashing? Or merely nice?

And what of a woman's heart? How has life handled her deepest desires?

The world kills a woman's heart when it tells her to be tough, efficient, and independent. She learns early that she must fight for herself because no one else will. There is no great adventure to be swept up into, only chores and errands and "to do" lists. And the arrows that pierce her heart over the years leave her doubting that she is the beauty in any story.

Can a woman live like that? Is that what little girls dreams about? Is that what *you* dreamed about?

Most women abandon those dreams of youth for some sort of competence to secure their places in an unkind world. They need to be bright and successful. They must be hard workers who can create a brilliant marketing campaign, throw an elegant dinner, and

cart the kids to soccer on time without losing the loveliness that every magazine tells them is possible to possess even during a downpour.

Sadly, Christianity has missed a woman's heart as well. Walk into most churches in America, look around, and ask yourself: what is a Christian woman? There is no

What if those deep desires in our hearts are telling us the truth, revealing to us the life we were meant to live?

doubt about it. You'd have to admit a Christian woman is *tired*. All we've offered the feminine soul is pressure to "be a good servant."

Ladies, which would you rather have said of you— that you are a "tireless worker," or that you are a "captivating woman?"

And men, which would you rather be said of you: "Harry? Sure I know him. He's a real sweet guy." Or, "Yes, I know all about Harry. He's a dangerous man . . . in a really good way."

I rest my case.

What happens when we abandon the deepest desires of our own heart is that we end up ruled by others' desires and demands.

Ann didn't know whether she should marry the man she was dating or not. They'd been dating for three years, but now she found herself lost as to what she should do. "Do you want to marry him?" I asked. "I don't know. I guess so. I'm not sure." Ann, a youth pastor, is a bright and energetic young lady whom people regularly turn to for counsel and encouragement. Ann always knows the "right" thing to do.

But now she was stumped. There was no "right" course to take. Her boyfriend was a committed Christian who loved her. She loved him, too. The problem was simply this: Ann had lived her entire life based on what was right and responsible, and had never made a decision based on her desire. So when the moment came for her to live out of her own desire, she was out of practice.

I have met so many people in the same position.

Charles is an attorney in his fifties who still doesn't know what he wants to be when he grows up. His wife left him last year because, as she explained to me, "he's dead inside."

THE DAMAGE OF

ABANDONED DESIRE

IS A LIFE LOST

UNTO ITSELF.

Paul doesn't know what to do now that college is over. He pursued good grades but left his heart behind in the process.

Jamie isn't sure if she should get married or stay single.

Barbara hates her job but hasn't the slightest idea what she'd do if she left.

Every one of them has tried to bury their heart and seek a safer life.

The damage of abandoned desire is a life lost unto itself.

Millions of souls drift through life without direction. They take their cues from others and live out scripts someone else wrote for them.

"This is the person you *ought* to be. This is what a good husband/wife/father/mother/Christian/friend ought to do." Fill in the blank from there. We learn to be responsible, sensitive, disciplined, faithful, diligent, dutiful, and so forth. Many of these are good qualities. The messengers who pressure us to adhere to such guidelines are well-intentioned, I have no doubt.

But the road to hell, as we recall, is paved with good

intentions. That they are a near total failure should seem obvious by now.

But what *if?*

What if those deep desires in our hearts are telling us the truth, revealing to us the life we were meant to live?

God gave us eyes so that we might see; he gave us ears that we might hear; he gave us wills that we might choose; and he gave us hearts that we might *live*. "I have come that they may have life," Jesus said, "and that they may have it more abundantly" (John 10:10). Some of us have never, ever heard that promise.

If you are to ever find yourself, you must find what God has set in your heart. Instead of asking what you ought to do to become a better man or woman, ask *what makes you come alive?* What stirs your heart?

When God created the masculine and the feminine hearts and set them within us, he offered us an invitation: Come and live out what I meant you to be.

TAKING UP
THE JOURNEY

WHAT DO YOU WANT?

--JESUS OF NAZARETH

IF YOU COULD DO

WHAT YOU'VE ALWAYS

WANTED TO DO,

WHAT WOULD IT BE?

S everal years ago I was thumbing through the introduction of a book when I ran across a passage that changed my life. It went like this:

Don't ask yourself what the world needs. Ask yourself what makes you come alive, and go do that, because what the world needs is people who have come alive.

I was struck dumb.

The page could have been Balaam's donkey, for all I was concerned. Suddenly my life up to that point made sense in a sickening sort of way—I realized I was living a script written for me by someone else.

All my life I had been asking the world to tell me what to do. Thank God it didn't work. Like David trying on Saul's armor, those other scripts never fit.

I set the volume down and walked out of that bookstore to find a life worth living.

I applied to graduate school and got accepted. That program would turn out to be far more than a career move: out of the transformation that took place there I became a writer, counselor, and speaker. My life changed, and as a result, so did the lives of many others down the road.

But I almost didn't go. You see, when I applied to school I didn't have a nickel to pay for it. I was married with three children and a mortgage, and that's the season when most men abandon their dreams. The risk just seems too great.

However, we must realize—God has rigged the world so that it only works when we embrace risk as the theme of our lives, when we live by faith. All attempts to find a safer life, to live by the expectations of others, just kill the soul in the end. That's not how we find life.

As Robert Frost wrote,

Two roads diverged in a wood, and I—
I took the one less traveled by,
And that has made all the difference.

So, let me now ask *you* the question:
If you had permission to do what you really want to

do, what would you do?

Don't ask *how*—that will cut your desire off at the knees. How is never the right question. How is a faithless question. It means "unless I can see my way clearly I won't

What is written in your heart?
What makes you come alive?

venture forth." When the angel told Zacharias that his ancient wife would bear him a son named John, Zacharias asked how and was struck dumb for it.

How is God's department: He is asking you *what*. What is written in your heart? What makes you come alive?

If you could do what you've always wanted to do, what would it be?

Discovering your heart's true desire takes a little time, especially if you've never asked yourself a question like this before. So let's start with something easier.

Let's go back to those movies you love. Pick three or four of your favorites and ask yourself, "What does the hero or heroine have that I would love to have? What is it about them and their lives that stirs my heart?"

I believe you'll find that the three core desires I mentioned are right there. Every man needs a battle to fight, an adventure to live, and a beauty to rescue. Every woman needs to be fought for, to be part of a great adventure, and to be the beauty in the story. Isn't that true—isn't that what makes those movies so deeply stirring?

You see, men and women are made in the image of God *as men* or *as women*. "So God created man in his own image; in the image of God he created him; male and female he created them" (Genesis 1:27). Now, we know God doesn't have a body, so the image can't be physical. Gender simply must be at the level of the soul, in the deep and everlasting places within us.

In other words, there is a masculine heart and a feminine heart, which in their own ways reveal to the world God's heart.

Look at the dreams of children. A pack of boys let loose in a wood soon launches a Civil War reenactment. A chorus of girls, upon discovering a trunk of skirts and dresses, begins to dance the Nutcracker Suite. This is deeper than culture; this is the image of God.

A friend and I were talking about our love of the

West and why he moved out here from the East Coast. Our conversation was stirred by the film *Legends of the Fall*, the story of three young men coming of age in the early 1900s on their father's ranch in Montana. Alfred, the eldest, is practical and cautious. He heads off to the big city to become a businessman and eventually, a politician. Yet something inside him dies. He becomes a hollow man. Samuel, the youngest, is still a boy in many ways, a tender child—literate, sensitive, timid. He is killed early in the film, and we know he was not ready for battle.

Then there is Tristan, the middle son. He is wild at heart. It is Tristan who embodies the West—he catches and breaks the wild stallion, fights the grizzly with a knife, and wins the beautiful woman.

I have yet to meet a man who wants to be Alfred or Samuel. I've yet to meet a woman who wants to marry one. There's a reason the American cowboy has taken on mythic proportions. He embodies a yearning every man knows from very young—to "go West," to find a place where he can be all he knows he was meant to be. He desires to be like author Walter Brueggeman's description of God: "wild, dangerous, unfettered and free."

The three desires essential to a woman's heart are not entirely different from a man's, and yet they remain distinctly feminine. Not every woman wants a battle to fight, but every woman yearns to be fought *for*. Listen to the longing of a woman's heart: She wants to be more than noticed—she wants to be *wanted*. She wants to be pursued. "I just want to be a priority to someone," a friend in her thirties told me.

And her dreams of a knight in shining armor coming to rescue her are not girlish fantasies; they are at the core of the feminine heart. So Zack sweeps up Paula in *An Officer and a Gentleman*; Friedrich comes back for Jo in *Little Women*, and Edward pledges his undying love for Elinor in *Sense and Sensibility*.

Every woman also wants an adventure to share. One of my wife's favorite films is *The Man from Snowy River*. She loves the scene where Jessica, the heroine, is rescued by Jim, her hero, and together they ride on horseback through the Australian wilderness. "I want to be Isabo in *Ladyhawk*," confessed another female friend. "To be cherished, pursued, fought for—yes. But also, I want to be strong and a part of the adventure."

And finally, every woman wants to have a beauty to unveil. Most women feel the pressure to be beautiful from very young, but that is not what I speak of. There is also a deep desire to *be* the beauty—simply and truly to be delighted in. Most little girls will remember playing dress up, or wedding day, or "twirling skirts." The child will put her pretty dress on, come into the living room and twirl. What she longs for is to capture her daddy's eye. My wife remembers standing on top of the coffee table as a girl of five or six, and singing her heart out. *Do you see me*, asks the heart of every girl? *And are you captivated by what you see?*

Now ask yourself, "What have I done with those desires?"

What have you done with the deep desires of your heart?

Because the truth is, those desires don't ever go away. If we do not find the life our heart was made for, if we abandon those desires and try to get on with our duties and obligations, those desires do not disappear.

They go underground.

DETOURS

We are half-hearted creatures, fooling about with drink and sex and ambition, when infinite joy is offered us, like an ignorant child who wants to go on making mud pies in a slum because he cannot imagine what is meant by the offer of a holiday at the sea. We are far too easily pleased.

— C. S. Lewis

WE LIVE SO DISTANT

NOW FROM EDEN, WE ARE

DESPERATE FOR LIFE, AND WE COME

TO BELIEVE THAT WE MUST ARRANGE

FOR IT AS BEST WE CAN,

OR NO ONE WILL.

I n fourteen hundred and ninety-two, as we all remember, Columbus sailed the ocean blue. But instead of opening a trade route to Asia, he unleashed something in the European imagination when he reported discovering a New World. What followed is amazing.

First, it was the Fountain of Youth.

Juan Ponce de Léon, a sailor with Christopher Columbus, heard of a mythical island called Bimini. A spring was reported to flow there, whose waters bestowed eternal youth. He obtained the backing of King Ferdinand to lead a party in search of the coveted fount. Failing to discover Bimini, Ponce de Léon stumbled upon Florida instead. He never found the Fountain of Youth, but he gave his life trying.

Then came El Dorado, the Lost City of Gold.

As conquistadors penetrated Central and South

America, they were enchanted by a legend telling of a kingdom of unfathomable riches, located somewhere in the Americas. The finder of this treasure would become wealthy beyond his wildest dreams. In 1535, Sebastián de Belalćazar began a three-year search for the fabled city through the jungles of Columbia. He failed, lost control of Peru, and died of fever.

You'd think the fates of Ponce de Leon and Sebastián de Belalcázar would dismay other adventurers. Not at all.

About the same time, Francisco Vázquez de Coronado was marching into northern Mexico, searching for the Seven Cities of Cibola (reputed to be flowing with gold). His expedition returned empty handed. After additional Spanish failures, Sir Walter Raleigh of England decided he'd give it a go. Not once, but twice he searched for El Dorado. On his second expedition in 1616, he violated the orders of King James I and attacked a Spanish settlement in Guyana. His son was killed, and Raleigh was beheaded upon his return home.

Are we really any different than those early explorers?

How come there are so many "sports widows," losing their husbands each weekend to the golf course or the TV?

Why are so many men addicted to sports? It's the biggest adventure many of them ever taste.

Why do so many others lose themselves in their careers? Same reason. I noticed recently that the *Wall Street Journal* advertises itself as "adventures in capitalism." I know guys who spend hours online trading stocks. There's a taste of excitement and risk to it, no question.

Many men fall into affairs not for love,
not even for sex, but, by their own admission,
for adventure.

And who can blame them? The rest of their life is chores and tedious routine.

It's no coincidence that many men fall into affairs not for love, not even for sex, but, by their own admission, for adventure.

Why is pornography the number one snare for men?

A man longs for a beauty, but without a fierce and passionate heart he cannot win her or keep her. So at a soul level he keeps his distance even though he is powerfully drawn to her. And privately, secretly, he turns to the imitation.

Pornography is so addictive because more than anything else in a lost man's life, it makes him *feel* like a man without requiring anything of him. The less a guy feels like a real man in the presence of a real woman, the more vulnerable he is to porn.

I hope you're getting the picture by now. If a man does not find those things for which his heart is made, he will look for them in some other way.

Why are so many men so angry?

They have no great battle to fight—just paying bills, enduring traffic, or getting the kids to behave. There's no place for a man to be a hero like William Wallace in *Braveheart,* so his fierce side goes underground. It simmers there in a hidden anger, waiting to erupt in a moment of frustration.

And what about women?

Who is making Danielle Steele rich? Romance stories have become the leading substitute of real intimacy for women. Remember, a woman is made to be pursued. But because so few women are actually pursued, they turn to impostors.

"Love can touch us one time and last for a lifetime." The theme music of *Titanic* played constantly in 1998—in grocery stores, over the radio, and on more than nine million copies of the CD. Celine Dion's hauntingly beautiful song was made all the more powerful by the central myth of our day—the idea that a special someone is out there, and if you can find him, his love will carry you for a lifetime.

How many women did this film motivate to keep searching for their own Golden One, their own Jack? Not long ago I received a phone call from a man I hadn't spoken with for a number of years. Through his sobs I gathered that his wife had left him and their children. He explained that she'd "met someone" on the Internet, and that relationship became her obsession. "It's my turn for love," was her explanation, "and I'm taking it."

"It's hard to be holy and passionate."

Cindy sighed as she said this. A bright young woman and a committed follower of Christ, she's also a bit more vulnerable to the boys than she'd like to be. It seems that the only way Cindy can keep from chasing after physical intimacy with a man is to bury herself in grad school. But the "run from desire" approach never works, and she soon finds herself leaving the books for another compromising situation. "Why can't I get beyond this?" she asked. "I'm praying and reading my Bible every day. But still I fall."

"What are you looking for?" I asked.

We sat in silence for a few minutes.

"I really don't know."

"That's your problem—you don't know. And so your unexamined desires rule you."

After a few moments she asked, "Is it pleasure? Excitement?" She was clueless. Despite her intelligence, I wasn't surprised that she had no clue as to why she couldn't break her addiction to boys.

As a rule, most of us live far from our heart's desire. So we're easily fooled by the impostors, the detours in our journey.

Women do the same thing with their hunger for adventure. Shopping, if you can believe it, has become the great adventure for women. It's not enough to find a gorgeous dress—you have to find it at a great deal. What do you make of the credit card debt in the United States? There are one and a half billion cards in circulation, with an average balance of $5,000 on each.

I was just looking at one of the cooking magazines my wife gets. Everything pictured is beautiful, delicious,

elegant. The kitchens portrayed are immaculate—there are no messes. The tables are sumptuous with their china place settings, brimming wine glasses, and tempting gourmet foods. Fresh flowers abound. The homes, of course, are lovely and spacious with an inspiring view. Everything is as it ought to be. Life is good. *You see*, the images whisper, *it can be done. Life is within your grasp.* And so the quest continues.

Don't be fooled by the apparent innocence of the object you've chosen to fill your heart's desire. We'll make an idol out of any good thing.

We're not the first generation to give idolatry a go; the spirit of it goes back at least as far as the Tower of Babel. But certainly mankind's options for idolatry have never been greater. The angel may bar our way back into Eden, but we're bound and determined to attain paradise on our own.

Wal-Mart is open twenty-four hours a day now, with a dozen restaurants and a multiplex theater nearby. More than one hundred channels are on the TV at home. Then there are computer games and the Internet. We've discovered gourmet coffee (tell your grandfather you're paying $5 for a cup), gourmet jelly beans, gourmet pop-corn—you name it.

We've nearly perfected our little pleasures. When the going gets tough, the tough go shopping, or fishing, or out to dinner. These things are all impostors—every one. But we're so taken by the dizzying array of choices, we never stop and take a good look at what we're doing.

Jenny fell in love in Ecuador. She wasn't looking for love, mind you. She had gone down to South America on a mission trip, so love came as a great surprise. Perhaps it was the romance of being in an exotic foreign land with a man who was charming, intelligent, and even a little bit dashing. Moreover, he was interested in her. His sincere questions, their shared laughter, and a mutual sense of purpose added to the powerful potion.

There was only one problem: he was married.

Jenny told me her story with a deep sense of shame. Nothing happened between them, but she had let her heart go farther than it should. She was embarrassed, humiliated. I wasn't surprised, not because Jenny is a flirt—far from it—but I know the story of her heart. Jenny is afraid of intimacy, and she's tried to live beyond

her desire for love. She's known the betrayal of love and carries the wounds to prove it. Of course she enjoyed his attention. We were made for that, remember? Like all of us, Jenny is designed for intimacy and adventure.

What made me angry was that she was about to draw the wrong conclusion, one the church often jumps to: Desire gets me into trouble. I must avoid it at all costs.

Jenny's story is not about the dangers of desire, but about the dangers of *disowned* desire. Just because she pretends she doesn't really want romance doesn't make the desire die. Instead, it goes underground, to surface somewhere else at some other time.

Poet David Whyte calls this the "devouring animal of our disowned desire." The danger of disowning desire is that it sets us up for a fall. We are unable to distinguish real life from a tempting imitation. Eventually, we find some imposter to give us a taste of the life we were meant to have.

When we lived in Eden, there was virtually no restriction on the pleasure around us. Our desire was innocent and fully satisfied. I cannot even imagine what five minutes in total bliss would be like. We had it all, and we threw it away. By mistrusting God's heart, by reaching to take control of what they wanted, Adam and Eve initiated a process in our hearts, a desperate grasping that can only be described as addiction.

Desire goes mad within us.

And that is why God must take away the heaven we create, or it will become our hell.

We might not think our efforts to attain a little of what we desire are anything like building heaven on earth.

God must take away the heaven we create,
or it will become our hell.

But some deep and tender place in us gets trapped in our false heaven—in those times and places where we have had a taste of the life we long for.

Addiction may seem like too strong a term to some of you. The woman who is serving so faithfully at church— surely there's nothing wrong with that? And who can blame the man who works late to provide for his family? Sure, you might look forward to the next meal more than most, and your hobbies can be a nuisance sometimes, but to call any of this an addiction seems to stretch the word a bit too far.

I have one simple response: give it up.

If you don't think you're secretly trying to fulfill your desires like any other addict, then prove it by letting go of the things that provide you with a sense of security, or comfort, or excitement, or relief. You will soon discover the tentacles of attachment deep in your own soul. There will be an anxiousness; you'll begin to think about work or food or golf even more. Withdrawal will set in. If you can make it a week or two out of sheer will power, you will feel a sadness growing in your soul, a deep sense of loss. Lethargy and a lack of motivation will follow.

We live so distant now from Eden, we are desperate for life, and we come to believe that we must arrange for it as best we can, or no one will.

So God must thwart us to save us.

God will take away our own plans for fulfilling our desires in order to draw us home to him, for only then can he give us what we truly desire without it hurting us.

TRUE NORTH

DELIGHT YOURSELF ALSO

IN THE LORD, AND HE SHALL

GIVE YOU THE DESIRES OF

YOUR HEART.

—PSALM 37:4

WE DON'T NEED MORE
FACTS AND WE CERTAINLY DON'T
NEED MORE THINGS TO DO—
WE NEED LIFE,
AND WE'VE BEEN LOOKING
FOR IT EVER SINCE WE
LOST PARADISE.

T his may come as a surprise to you: Christianity is not an invitation to become a moral person.

It is not a program for getting us in line or for reforming society. Christianity does have a powerful effect upon our lives, but when transformation comes, it is always the *after-effect* of something else—something at the level of our hearts.

And so at its core, Christianity begins with an invitation to *desire*.

"Come, all you who are thirsty, come to the waters;
and you who have no money, come, buy and eat!
Come, buy wine and milk
    without money and without cost.
Why spend money on what is not bread,
    and your labor on what does not satisfy?

Listen, listen to me, and eat what is good,
and your soul will delight in the richest of fare."

Isaiah 55:1–2, NIV

To the weary, Jesus speaks of rest. To the lost, he speaks of finding the way. Again and again, Jesus takes people back to their desires.

"Ask, and it will be given to you; seek, and you will find; knock, and it will be opened to you" (Matthew 7:7). These are outrageous words, provocative words. Ask, seek, knock—these are words that invite and *arouse* desire.

What do you *want*?

But that's not how most people hear the invitation of Christianity nowadays.

Christianity usually is presented as being about knowledge and performance. First, we are given a bunch of facts. We learn where the Philistines originated, and how much a *drachma* would be worth today, and all sorts of things from "the original Greek." We learn about correct doctrine. Yet the information presented couldn't be less relevant to our deepest desires.

Then we are told to get our behavior in line, one way

or another. Regardless of where we go to church, there is nearly always an unspoken "list" as to what we shouldn't do (typically rather long) and a list of what we may do—usually much shorter, mostly religious activity that seems unrelated to our deepest desires and leaves us exhausted.

And this, we are told, is the "good news." Know the right thing, do the right thing. This is life? When this doesn't excite us, we suspect we are not spiritual enough. Perhaps once we have kept the lists long enough, we will understand.

We don't need more facts and we certainly don't need more things to do—we need *life,* and we've been looking for it ever since we lost paradise.

Most of us never really let this sink in: Once upon a time we lived in paradise. Really.

Mankind lived in a world full of beauty and intimacy and adventure. Our hearts were made to live in that habitat. Picture Maui at sunset with your dearest love. There was true happiness—no pain, no sorrow, no suffering. The human story does not begin with sin, it begins in the garden of delight. It begins with our own hearts full of glory and goodness, set in a world of exciting exploration, together.

The desires of our heart tell us this is true. We know there is a better life than the one we have. When the Scripture tells us that God has set eternity in the heart of every person (Ecclesiastes 3:11), we need to stop and ask ourselves where? Where in my heart is eternity written? The answer is, in your *desires*.

As scientist and philosopher Blaise Pascal asked, "What can this incessant craving mean, unless there was once a happiness belonging to man, of which only the faintest traces remain?"

But we mistrusted God's heart toward us. There was

Jesus came, not to lay heavy burdens on our backs, but to return us to our true Father.

one tree in the garden God told us not to reach for—only one. Satan whispered to our hearts a deep suspicion. "God is holding out on you," he said. "He's not really interested in your happiness. You've got to take matters into your own hands, get control of things, arrange for your own happiness." We believed the lie, and paradise was lost.

And now we too are lost, and far from home.

And this is why Jesus came—not to lay heavy burdens on our backs, but to return us to our true Father and our true home. In his own words, Jesus said, "I have come that they may have life, and that they may have it more abundantly" (John 10:10).

"If you are thirsty, come to me! If you believe in me, come and drink! For the Scriptures declare that rivers of living water will flow out from within" (John 7:37–38 NLT).

Jesus did not say, "I have come to threaten you into line," nor "I have come to exhaust you with a long list of demands." Not even, "I have come primarily to forgive you." But simply, *my purpose is to bring you life in all its fullness.*

Do you recall the story of the Samaritan woman, whom Jesus meets at a well one hot afternoon?

She has come alone to draw water during the heat of the day, when her chances are good that she won't run into anyone. You see, her sexual lifestyle has earned her a "reputation." She's on her sixth lover, and so she'd rather bear the scorching rays of the sun than face the searing words of the "decent" women of the town who come at evening to draw water. She succeeds in avoiding

the women, but runs into God instead.

Now, what does Jesus choose to talk to her about—her immorality? No, he speaks to her about her *thirst*.

"If you knew the generosity of God and who I am, you would be asking me for a drink, and I would give you fresh, living water" (John 4:10 MESSAGE).

Remarkable. He doesn't preach about purity; he doesn't even mention it, except to say that he knows what her life has been like. "You have had five husbands, and the one whom you now have is not your husband" (John 4:18). In other words, let's talk about your heart's real thirst, since the life you've chosen obviously isn't working.

And so Jesus awakens our desire, because it is what he came to address. When we abandon desire we no longer hear or understand what Jesus is saying.

We've been told that desire is the enemy. After all, desire is the single major hindrance to the goal—getting us in line. And so we are told to kill desire, and call it sanctification.

But God is not the enemy of desire. "Delight yourself also in the LORD," the psalmist tells us, "and he shall give you the desires of your heart" (Psalm 37:4). After all, God is the one who made these deep hearts within us, created us as men and women with these deep longings. And though we turned our backs on him, he pursued us, called us back to his own good heart, and intends to bring us Life again.

This is why holiness is not deadness; it is passion. It is being *more* attuned to our desires, to what we were truly made for and therefore what we truly want. Our problem is that we've grown quite used to seeking our life in all kinds of things other than God. As psychiatrist and author Gerald May says,

> God wants to be our perfect lover, but instead we seek perfection in human relationships and are disappointed when our lovers cannot love us perfectly. God wants to provide our ultimate security, but we seek our safety in power and possessions and then we find we must continually worry about them. We seek satisfaction of our spiritual longing in a host of ways that may have very little to do with God.

We don't really know what will satisfy.

This is where the commands of God are our help. Everything in you may be saying, "But you don't understand. I want to eat that whole box of chocolates, or sleep with my boyfriend, or let my anger really fly. That's what really seems like life to me right now."

God says, "I know you do, but it'll kill you in the end. What you think is life, is not. That's not the comfort, nor the love, nor the significance you are seeking. You'll wind up destroying yourself." The commands of God become our tutor in healing our desire. Only because we've strayed so far from home do we have to be told not to lie and cheat and murder each other.

So the first command comes first. God tells us to

Contentment is not freedom from desire, but freedom of desire.

love him with all our heart and with all our soul, with all our mind and all our strength. It's not a burden but a rescue, a trail out of the jungles of desire.

When we don't look for God as our true life, our desire for him spills over into our other desires, giving them a primacy and urgency they were never intended to bear.

We become desperate, grasping and arranging and

worrying over all kinds of things, and once we get them, they end up ruling us.

It's the difference between *wants* and *needs*.

All we truly need is God. Prone to wander from him, we find we need all sorts of other things. Our desire becomes insatiable because we've taken our longing for the Infinite and placed it upon the finite. God saves us from the whole crazy mess by turning our hearts back to him.

You may have heard an orchestra tuning up before a concert. It sounds like total chaos—oboes, cellos, French horns, dozens of instruments all sounding off, everyone doing their own thing. This is how our desires seem most of the time. But then the first violin plays a long high C, and all the other instruments join in. They become focused, centered, ready to perform.

This is what happens with the chaos of our desires when we turn our souls to God in worship. When we delight in him, he heals our false desires and our souls come true in the light of their Creator.

And now for the deepest secret of all.

Contentment is not freedom *from* desire, but freedom *of* desire. To be content is not pretending that everything

is the way you wish it would be, nor is it acting as though you have no wishes. Rather, it is no longer being ruled by your desires.

We are on a journey of desire. But we are not yet home.

The fact is, at this point in our journey, we have only three options:

> to be alive and thirsty,
> to be dead in our soul,
> to be addicted.

There are no other choices.

Most of the world lives in addiction; most of the church has chosen deadness. But the Christian is called to the life of holy longing.

You can be satisfied; you just can't be sated. There is great joy in a glass of cabernet; the whole bottle is another story. Intimate conversation satisfies a different thirst, but how awful to try and arrange for it again the next night, and the night after that. The Israelites tried to hoard the manna—and it crawled with maggots.

Our soul's insatiable desire becomes a tyrant when it demands its fill here and now, through the otherwise beautiful and good gifts of our lives. For God does grant us so much of our heart's desire, as we delight in him. "You open Your hand and satisfy the desire of every living thing" (Psalm 145:16). Not always, not on demand, but certainly more than we deserve. God delights to give good gifts to his beloved.

How then shall we not lose heart? If we hang onto our desire, how do we keep from being consumed by it?

The secret is known to all of us, although we might have forgotten that we know it. Who wants to fill up with

God delights to give good gifts to his beloved.

snacks on Thanksgiving Day? Who goes out to buy presents for themselves on Christmas Eve? Does anyone in their right mind look for someone to date at their wedding rehearsal? When we are convinced that something delicious is about to be ours, it frees us to live in expectation and it draws us on in anticipation.

But nearly every person I have spoken with has an

idea that eternity is an unending church service. After all, the Bible says that the saints worship God in heaven, and without giving it much more thought we have settled on an image of the never-ending sing-along in the sky—one great hymn after another, forever and ever, amen.

And our heart sinks. That's it? That's the good news?

Then we sigh and feel guilty that we are not more "spiritual." And so we lose heart, and we turn once more to the present to find what life we can. Eternity ends up having no bearing on our search for life whatsoever. It feels like the end of the search. As C. S. Lewis said, *we can only hope for what we desire.* How can the never-ending church service in the sky be better than a month in Hawaii with someone you love?

But what if you knew in your heart that the life you prize was just around the corner? Remember, when God "set eternity in our hearts" he wrote it on our desires. We long for beauty, intimacy, and adventure, and that is exactly what is coming to us in the fullness of God's kingdom. Desire cannot live without hope.

We must *know* that true life is about to be ours in all its fullness.

DESIRE'S
HOMECOMING

SEE! THE WINTER IS PAST;

THE RAINS ARE OVER AND GONE.

FLOWERS APPEAR ON THE EARTH;

THE SEASON OF SINGING HAS COME,

—SONG OF SOLOMON 2:11–12, NIV

OUR HEART'S

DEEPEST DESIRES

WILL HAVE FINALLY

COME HOME.

There's a reason most people don't live with a lot of hope. Most of us have never *really* heard the fabulous news Jesus brought with him.

Oh, I know—we've heard something about our sin, and the cross, and maybe a little about forgiveness. We've heard about being good little boys and girls until we die and go to heaven. But you know what? That's not the message Jesus brought. Not really.

Jesus preached far more than the gospel of sin management. He came to announce the coming of "the kingdom of God."

> *And Jesus went about all Galilee, teaching in their synagogues, preaching the gospel of the kingdom* (Matthew 4:23).

"The time is fulfilled, and the kingdom of God is at hand. Repent, and believe in the gospel" (Mark 1:15).

He went through every city and village, preaching and bringing the glad tidings of the kingdom of God (Luke 8:1).

After his suffering, he showed himself to these men and gave many convincing proofs that he was alive. He appeared to them over a period of forty days and spoke about the kingdom of God (Acts 1:3, NIV).

What exactly is this kingdom of God? What does it mean for our lives?

A kingdom is a realm where the king's word has full sway. What the king desires is what happens. God's kingdom come means that his will is done "on *earth* as it is in heaven." Now in heaven, things are not stained or broken; everything is as it was meant to be. Think for a moment of the wonder of this. Isn't every one of our sorrows on earth the result of things *not* being as they were meant to be?

And so when the kingdom of God comes to earth, wonderful things begin to unfold.

Look at the evidence: watch what happens to people

as they are touched by the kingdom of God through Jesus. As he went about "preaching the gospel of the kingdom," Jesus was also "healing all kinds of sickness and all kinds of disease among the people" (Matthew 4:23). When he "spoke to them about the kingdom of God," he "healed those who had need of healing" (Luke 9:11). A direct connection is made here.

All the miracles of Jesus are illustrations for the sermon.

What happens when we find ourselves in the kingdom of God? The lame leap to their feet and start doing a jig. The deaf buy themselves stereo equipment. The blind

The kingdom of God brings restoration.
Life is restored to what it was meant to be.

---

go to the movies. The dead show up for dinner.

Human brokenness in all its forms is healed. The kingdom of God brings *restoration*. Life is restored to what it was meant to be.

Remember how our address used to be paradise, and that our hearts know there is a better life we were meant to enjoy? That's what "heaven" is all about.

Only, we don't disappear up into a wispy heaven and play harps on a cloud.

"In the beginning," back in Eden, all of creation was pronounced good, because all of creation was exactly as God meant for it to be. For it to be good again is not for it to be destroyed, but healed, renewed, brought back to its goodness. Those glimpses we see in the miracles of Jesus were the first fruits. When he announces the full coming of the kingdom, Jesus says,

"Behold, I make all things new" (Revelation 21:5).

He does not say, "I am making all new things."

He means that the things that have been so badly broken will be restored and then some. "You mean I'll get a new pair of glasses?" my son Sam asked. "Or do you mean I'll get a new pair of eyes, so I won't need glasses?" What do you think? Jesus didn't hand out crutches to the lame.

And it's not just a new heaven, but a new earth (Isaiah 65:17; Revelation 21:1)!

The created world itself can hardly wait for what's coming next. Everything in creation is being more or less held back. God reins it in until both creation and

all the creatures are ready and can be released at
the same moment into the glorious times ahead.
Meanwhile, the joyful anticipation deepens
(Romans 8:19–21, MESSAGE).

How wondrous this will be: if creation can be so breathtaking now, what will it be like when it's released to its full glory?

Think about the return of spring for a moment. (Those of you who've lived in a winter climate will really understand this.)

Here in the Rocky Mountains, the flowers are pretty much gone in September. The first of October, the aspens start turning gold and begin to drop their leaves. Come November all is gray. The coming of winter has its joys to anticipate, like Thanksgiving and Christmas, but after the New Year, the season grows dreary. Through February and March the earth remains lifeless in brown and gray tones. Winter drags through April. While the azaleas are coming out full glory in Atlanta, we're still shoveling snow. It's too long!

But then, suddenly, the world is alive again, transformed. The trees are green. The birds are back. It all happens so quickly—in the twinkling of an eye.

The return of spring brings such relief and joy and anticipation. Life has returned, and with it sunshine, warmth, color, and the long summer days of adventure. We break out the lawn chairs and the grills. We tend the garden and drink in all the beauty. We head off for vacations. Isn't this what we most deeply long for? To leave the winter of the world behind and find ourselves suddenly in the open meadows of summer?

Spring is God's word to us: "The winter will soon be past, spring will come and then summer behind it. But this is a summer that will never pass away. Look, I am making everything new!"

Now *that* is really good news.

The restoration of God's good creation not only answers our heart's longing for beauty, but for adventure as well.

Jesus told a story about a landowner who went away on a journey. He was a nobleman who went to "a far country to receive for himself a kingdom" (Luke 19:12). Upon his return, he rewarded the faithful members of his staff in a way that at first seems, well, like no reward at all. "You were faithful over a few things, I will make you ruler over many things" (Matthew 25:21). Luke's version states it like this: "Because you were faithful in a very little, have authority over ten cities" (Luke 19:17).

That is their bonus? More to do? Wouldn't a vacation make a better reward? My boys clean their rooms so they can go out and play, not so they can clean the rest of the house. Yet Jesus thinks that he is sharing something delightful with us. For the landowner then says, "Enter into the joy of your lord" (Matthew 25:21).

Think about God's work for minute—what brings him joy?

> *He wraps himself in light as with a garment;*
> *He stretches out the heavens like a tent*
> *And lays the beams of his upper chambers on*
> *   their waters.*
> *He makes the clouds his chariot*
> *And rides on the wings of the wind.*
> *He makes springs pour water into the ravines;*
> *It flows between the mountains.*
> *They give water to all the beasts of the field;*

The wild donkeys quench their thirst.

The birds of the air nest by the waters;

They sing among the branches.

He waters the mountains from his upper chambers;

The earth is satisfied by the fruit of his work.

He makes grass grow for the cattle,

And plants for man to cultivate?

Bringing forth food from the earth:

Wine that gladdens the heart of man,

Oil to make his face shine,

And bread that sustains his heart.

Psalm 104:2–3, 10–14, NIV

The only way to describe God's creative work is *extravagant*.

Thunderclouds gather over the prairies, and afterward he scatters wildflowers as far as the eye can see. He fills the oceans with orcas and urchins and only he knows what. A single maple leaf is woven with greater intricacy than the finest French lace—even though it will fall with the winds of autumn. New sunsets are painted and swept away each night. What magnificent generosity! No composer ever gave so many free concerts.

As poet and pastor George MacDonald said, "Gloriously wasteful, O my Lord, art thou!" You don't suppose God experiences his part in running the universe as drudgery, do you? Do Margot Fonteyn and Rudolf Nureyev love to dance? Does Michael Jordon love to play basketball? So God loves his work.

And it is this life, with all its joyful creativity and power and unending happiness that God says he is going to share with us. This is "the joy of your lord" that we are to enter. It rather beats the never-ending sing-along, wouldn't you say?

For we long to find our place in the world, caring for and developing creation in all its diverse potential. Gardeners dream of a spot of ground with rich soil and no weeds or sow bugs. They shall have it. Architects long to build their own designs, and not merely carry out the plans of another. They shall do it. We will all find our place in God's great kingdom and share the adventure together.

We were made for this.

We'll be filled with beauty, for the earth shall be

restored. And we'll have more than our share of adventure, for we will all live out the gifts God has given us and take care of his kingdom. But what about our deepest desire of all—what about *intimacy*?

*The exotic intimacy of sex was given to us
as a picture of something else, something truly
out of this world.*

Jesus says the new kingdom begins not with a church service, but with a feast. And it's not just any kind of feast—it's a wedding feast.

No union on earth is like the consummation of the love between a man and woman. No other connection reaches as deeply as this oneness was meant to; no other passion is nearly so intense. The passion spousal love evokes is instinctive, irrational, intense, and dare I say, immortal. As the Song of Solomon says,

> *Love is as strong as death,*
> *its jealousy unyielding as the grave.*
> *It burns like blazing fire, like a mighty flame.*

Many waters cannot quench love;

rivers cannot wash it away.

Song of Solomon 8:6–7, NIV

Small wonder that many people experience sexual passion as their highest transcendence on this earth. This is not simply about hormones and sex drives—it's about a deeper reality, a desire for something glorious.

The exotic intimacy of sex was given to us as a picture of something else, something truly out of this world.

After creating this stunning portrait of a total union—the man and woman becoming one—God turns the universe on its head when he tells us that this is what *he* is seeking with *us*.

In fact, Paul says it is *why* God created gender and sexuality and marriage—to serve as a living metaphor. He quotes Genesis, then takes it to the tenth degree:

> *"For this reason a man shall leave his father and mother and be joined to his wife, and the two*

shall become one flesh. This is a great mystery, but I speak concerning Christ and the church" (Ephesians 5:31–32).

What we have sought, what we have tasted in part with our earthly love, we will come face to face with in our True Love. God is the source of all masculine power; God is also the fountain of all feminine allure. He is the wellspring of everything that has ever romanced your heart—the thundering strength of a waterfall, the delicacy of a flower, the stirring

What we have tasted in part with our earthly love, we will come face to face with in our True Love.

capacity of music, the richness of a fine wine. The masculine and feminine that fill all creation come from the same heart.

The incompleteness that we seek to relieve in the embrace of our earthly love is never fully healed. The union does not last, whatever the poets and pop artists may say. Morning comes and we've got to get out of bed and off to our day, incomplete once more. But oh, to have our incompleteness healed forever, to drink deeply from that fount of which we've only had a sip, to dive into that sea in which we have only waded.

And there is more.

God has created a kingdom so rich in love that he should not be our all, but rather, that others should be precious to us as well.

Even in Eden, before the fall, while Adam walked in Paradise with his God, even then God said "It is not good that man should be alone" (Genesis 2:18). He gives to us the joy of community, of family and friends to share in the sacred romance. Is it not the nature of true love to be generous in love? This is part of the reason married couples long to have children; they want others to share in their happiness.

Many of you have lost a parent, a spouse, even a child. This is one of our deepest of all griefs, to lose someone we love.

And it will be one of our greatest joys, to have that person restored to us again.

When Jesus rose from the dead, his friends recognized him as Jesus. He didn't become an angel, or a spirit; he didn't disappear forever. The Jesus they had known and loved, they could never ever lose again. His life had become inextinguishable. And ours shall be as well.

The naked intimacy, the real knowing that we'll enjoy with God, we shall enjoy with one another. As George MacDonald wrote, "I think we shall be able to pass into and through each other's very souls as we please, knowing each other's thought and being, along with our own, and so being *like* God." My friend Brent Curtis used to call it multiple intimacy without promiscuity. It is what the ancients meant by the Communion of Saints.

All of the joy that awaits us in the sea of God's love will be multiplied over and over as we share with each other in the Grand Affair. Poet John Donne captures this so beautifully:

> *All mankind is of one author, and is one volume;*
> *when one man dies, one chapter is not torn out of the*
> *book, but translated into a better language; and every*
> *chapter must be so translated; God employs several*
> *translators: some pieces are translated by age, some by*
> *sickness, some by war, some by justice; but God's hand*
> *is in every translation; and His hand shall bind up*

all our scattered leaves again, for that library where
every book shall open to one another.

Imagine the stories we'll hear and all the questions that will finally have answers. "What were you thinking when you drive the old Ford onto the ice?" "Did you hear that Betty and Dan got back together? But of course you did." "How come you never told us about your time in the war?" "Did you ever know how much I loved you?" And the answers won't be brief replies, but story after story, a feast of wonder and laughter and glad tears.

As author Dallas Willard reminds us, "The life we now have, as the persons we now are, will continue in the universe in which we now exist."

Our heart's deepest desires will have finally come home.

EMBRACING
THE JOURNEY

WHEN I NO MORE CAN STIR MY

SOUL TO MOVE, AND LIFE IS BUT THE

ASHES OF A FIRE; WHEN I CAN BUT

REMEMBER THAT MY HEART ONCE

USED TO LIVE AND LOVE,

LONG AND ASPIRE—WAKE IN ME . . .

BOUNDLESS DESIRE.

—GEORGE MACDONALD

WHEN THE GOING

GETS ROUGH,

WE'RE GOING NOWHERE

WITHOUT DESIRE.

W e are faced with a decision that grows with urgency each passing day: will we leave our small, safe stories behind to follow God into the fulfillment of our desires? The choice to become a pilgrim of the heart can happen any day, and we can begin our journey from any place. We are here, the time is now, and the romance is always unfolding.

A sacred romance calls to us every moment of our lives. It whispers to us on the wind, invites us through the laughter of good friends, reaches out to us through the touch of someone we love. We've heard it in our favorite music, sensed it at the birth of our first baby, been drawn to it while watching the shimmer of a sunset on the ocean.

It is present even in times of great personal suffering—the illness of a child, the loss of a marriage, the death of a friend. Something calls to us through moments like these and rouses an inconsolable longing for intimacy, beauty, and adventure.

This longing is the most powerful part of any human personality. It fuels our search for meaning, for wholeness, for a sense of being truly alive.

And the voice that calls to us in this place is none other than the voice of God.

You see, the choice before us is *not* to "make life happen."

The choice before us is a choice to enter into the adventure God sets before us.

So much of the journey forward requires letting go of all that once brought us life. In a way it means we stop

The choice before us is a choice to enter into the adventure God sets before us.

---

pretending that life is better than it is, that we are happier than we are, that the false selves we present to the world are really us.

We respond to our deepest desires, the longing for another life.

In *Pilgrim's Progress*, John Bunyan's seventeenth-century allegory of the sacred romance, a man comes to see his own story as he has never seen it before, and he is appalled by it. He longs for true life, and he knows that to stay where he is means death.

Against the protestations of family and friends, he launches on a remarkable adventure. "I saw in my dream," Bunyan wrote, "That this man began to run." But as Bunyan tells it, "he had not run far from his own door" before the characters in the man's small story, his old life, ran to fetch him back, crying out all the threats and excuses they could imagine.

"But the man put his fingers in his ears, and ran on, crying, 'Life! Life! Eternal life!'"

Pilgrim begins his adventure towards redemption with a two-fold turning— a turning *away* from addiction and a turning *toward* desire.

When the going gets rough, we're going nowhere without desire.

And the going will get rough. The world, the minions of darkness, and your own double-mindedness are all set against you. Just try coming alive, try living from your heart for the sacred romance and watch how the world responds.

People will hate you for your new life and will strive to force you back into the comfort of the way things were. Your passion will disrupt them, because it reminds them of their own neglected hearts. If they can't convince you to live in the safer places that they've chosen, they will try intimidation. If that fails, they'll try to kill you— if not literally, then at the level of the soul.

This is no easy journey we're taking. That's why the Scriptures admonish us to use Jesus as our example:

> *Let us fix our eyes on Jesus, the author and perfector of our faith, who for the joy set before him endured the cross, scorning its shame, and sat down at the right hand of the throne of God. Consider him, who endured such opposition from sinful men, so that you will not grow weary and lose heart.* (Hebrews 12:2–3, NIV).

Far more than the character in Bunyan's allegory, Jesus ran because he *wanted* to, not because he had to or because the Father told him to. He ran "for the joy set before him," which means he ran out of *desire*. To

use the familiar phrase, his heart was fully in it.

You may recall the movie *Chariots of Fire*, which tells the story of two Olympic runners: Eric Liddell and Harold Abrams. Both are passionate about running, but in very different ways. Abrams runs in order to prove something: he is a cheerless man whose whole life is motivated by ought, by duty, by law. Liddell runs because he can't help it. "When I run," he says, "I feel God's pleasure." He knows a freedom of heart that Abrams can only watch from a distance.

Abrams uses discipline to subdue and kill his heart. Liddell is so freed by grace that when he runs, Abram says, "he runs like a wild animal—he unnerves me." "Where," Liddell asks, "does the power come from to see the race to its end? It comes from within."

It comes from desire.

Sadly, many of us have been led to feel that somehow we ought to want less, not more. We have this sense that we should atone for our longings, apologize that we feel such deep desire. Shouldn't we be more content?

Perhaps, but contentment is not wanting *less*; that's the easy way out. Anybody can look holy if he's killed his heart; the real test is to have your heart burning within you and have the patience to enjoy what there is now to enjoy, while waiting with eager anticipation for the feast to come.

Contentment can only happen as we *increase* desire, let it run toward its fulfillment, and carry us along with it.

Yes, there might be times when we must rely on a sense of duty. But in the end, if that's all we have, we will never make it. Our hero, Jesus, is the example. He's run on before us and he's made it. His life assures us that running to fulfillment can be done, but only through passionate desire for the joy set before *us*.

Let me summarize:

- Your heart's desire is *good,* for it was given to you by God and is meant to lead you to the life God meant for you.

- No, not every desire that occurs to you is good. We've all been fooled by impostors.

- But the way towards true life is not abandoning

desire, but by entering more deeply into your heart's longings.

- You can embrace desire with hope, knowing that very soon your heart will find its true home.

- And in the meantime, as you delight yourself in the truest Desire of your heart, Christ gives enough to satisfy you on the way and increase your thirst for the fullness yet to come.

Once we realize what a precious thing this is, our heart's desire, we must see that to guard it is worth our

We must be serious about our happiness.

---

all. To neglect it is foolishness. To kill it is suicide. To allow it to wander aimlessly, to be trapped by the impostors, is disaster.

Let's revisit the story Jesus told of the man who entrusted three of his servants with the equivalent of millions of dollars (literally, "talents") urging them to handle his affairs well while he was away. When he returned, the man listened eagerly to their reports.

The first two fellows went out into the marketplace and doubled their investments. As a result, they were handsomely rewarded. The third servant was not so fortunate. His gold was taken from him, and he was thrown into "the outer darkness. There will be weeping and gnashing of teeth" (Matthew 25:30). My goodness. Why? All he did was bury the money under the porch until his master's return. Most of us would probably agree with the path the third servant chose—it's safe. But his reasoning is faulty. Listen to how he explains his choice to his master:

> *"Sir, I know you are a hard man, harvesting crops you didn't plant and gathering crops you didn't cultivate. I was afraid I would lose your money, so I hid it"* (Matthew 25:24–25, NLT).

He was afraid of the master, whom he saw as a hard man. He didn't trust his master's heart. The issue isn't capital gains—it's what we think of God.

When we bury our desires we are saying the same thing: "God, I don't dare desire because I fear you. I think you are hard-hearted." Killing desire

may look like sanctification, but it's really godlessness— our way of handling life without God. Those who trust God are willing to risk desire.

Jesus teaches about how God answers prayer by telling the story of a persistent widow who wasn't getting the justice she deserved from a belligerent judge. The woman wins her case because she refuses to let up, and Jesus uses her as a picture of unrelenting desire. He urges us not only to ask, but to keep on asking. And then he ends the parable by wondering out loud, "But when I, the Son of Man, return, how many will I find who have faith?" (Luke 18:8, NLT).

We know in our hearts the connection he is making, though we haven't admitted it to ourselves.

To live with desire is to choose vulnerability over self-protection; to admit our desire and seek help beyond ourselves is even more vulnerable still. It is an act of trust.

Those who know their desire, and embrace it, looking to a good God to fulfill their desire—they are the ones who live by faith.

MORE INFORMATION

If *Dare to Desire* has touched your heart,
you might like to read some of John Eldredge's other books,
all available from Thomas Nelson Publishers.

THE JOURNEY OF DESIRE:
Searching for the Life We've Only Dreamed Of
Most of the content from *Dare to Desire* was drawn from this
full-length book, which provides a deeper look into your God-given
desires, and shows you how to search again for the life
you once dreamed of.

THE SACRED ROMANCE:
Drawing Closer to the Heart of God,
with Brent Curtis

WILD AT HEART:
Discovering the Secret of a Man's Soul

To contact John regarding his seminars and retreats:

John Eldredge
RANSOMED HEART MINISTRIES
P.O. Box 51065, Colorado Springs, CO 80949-1065

www.sacredromance.com